CONTENTS

KT-117-012

BLUFF YOUR WAY IN
PERSONAL FINANCE

ANNE GORDON

RR

RAVETTE PUBLISHING

Published by Ravette Publishing Limited
P.O. Box 296
Horsham
West Sussex RH13 8FH

Telephone: (01403) 711443
Fax: (01403) 711554

Series Editor – Anne Tauté

Cover design – Jim Wire, Quantum
Printing & binding – Cox & Wyman Ltd.
Production – Oval Projects Ltd.

The Bluffer's Guides™ series is based
on an original idea by Peter Wolfe.

The Bluffer's Guides™, Bluffer's™
and Bluff Your Way™ are Trademarks.

An Oval Project
for Ravette Publishing.

The author and the Bluffer's Guides™
disclaim responsibility for all consequences
of anyone acting on, or refraining from acting
on any information or opinion contained in
this book, including omission, commission
and fantasy.

INTRODUCTION

How you spend, save, borrow or invest is 'Personal Finance'. Once a simple household concept, involving money under mattresses and pennies in piggybanks, personal finance has been hijacked by financial institutions, such as banks and building societies.

These have secured their markets by tying up customers with many layers of obfuscation which need to be understood. There are also words.

Some are pure jargon, like 'OEICs' and 'SERPS'. Others are ordinary everyday words with new meanings: 'spread' isn't straight from the fridge and 'pups' are not small dogs. Many signal the opposite of what you'd expect: 'GUARANTEED' in big letters warns you to look carefully at the small print; 'interest' is usually dull, and 'trusts' invariably suspect.

Then commonplace words are roped together, and change their identity. Money and purchase are easy to understand individually, but 'money purchase'? Or 'earnings cap', 'contribution holiday', and 'tied agent'?

This guide shows you how these terms are used and helps you unpick their meanings. Then, when a financial adviser walks off with your money, you will know what you can expect in return. After all, few people book a holiday without knowing where they are going, with whom or for how long, and what their chances are of contracting marriage or malaria.

So if you don't want to send your money on a mystery cruise, get to know the lie of the land and learn the language correctly. At the least, it allows you to outbluff those who might otherwise bamboozle you. At best, it might pay for the trip of a lifetime.

FINANCIAL INSTITUTIONS

Financial institutions never die, they simply change their form. Building societies buy insurance companies, insurance companies set up banks, and banks are moving into fund management. This has increased their size and efficiency – but also turned them into faceless monoliths.

Unfortunately people don't like doing business with faceless monoliths, so the institutions mask the change by:

1. Spending most of their efficiency savings building a brand identity and advertising it. They want their brand to pass into the language, like Biro, Hoover and Semtex. This is of course a two-edged sword: both the Mafia and the Borgias have powerful brands.

2. Changing their collective name from 'financial institutions' to 'financial services'. This makes them appear customer-led and consumer-facing, focusing on client care rather than corporate profits. If you believe this, read the shareholders' Annual Report.

3. Moving in with you. The internet imports financial institutions into the home. And you wouldn't want to share your bedroom with a faceless monolith, would you?

Banks

Banks have a strong brand image. They are big, secure and reliable – you can bank on them. Unless of course they go bust, like BCCI, or invest uncontrollably in derivatives, like Barings.

You can improve your position by:

a. Moving. People are more likely to change their partner than their bank. This suits the banks, who are inertia-dependent. But lots of other financial institutions want your business, so it can be a distinct advantage to be promiscuous rather than staying where you are and being taken for granted.

b. Threatening to move. This may be enough to improve your position. Losing customer accounts is bad for a manager's performance related pay. Threats work even for shopaholics with overdrafts. Banks make a fortune from overdrafts.

c. Transferring most of your money. Even threats are rarely sufficient to increase the derisory interest on your current account. Leave only enough money to pay the monthly bills, and transfer the rest: you deserve a more interesting time. Perfect savers develop money-movement into an art form.

d. Becoming a shareholder. Most of the profit that should be in your account is in their pockets. If you can't beat them, join the shareholder register.

Life Insurance Companies

Or, more accurately, 'death insurance companies'. You pay them money (in the form of **premiums**) and they give your friends and relatives a lump sum when you die – unless you cheat by committing suicide too soon.

Because people live longer now, life companies have branched out into pensions, long term savings and policies which pay out if you get sick – predictably called 'health' insurance.

An insurance company may sell **with-profits** policies, or **unit-linked** policies. A with-profits policy means that your money goes into a big pot along with everyone else's. When your pay-day comes, the actuary looks into the pot and decides how much you should have. This can only be a finger in the air job – sometimes two fingers in the air.

If you have a unit-linked policy, the company links you up with certain specific assets. What you get at the end of the policy term depends on how well these assets have performed. Unit-linking is more accurate than with-profits, and if your assets have done well your returns should reflect this. But if you've been tied to Uruguayan uranium mines, you might have preferred a with-profits fund where you could have shared the pain.

You can improve your position by:

a. Never buying without researching the market first.
b. Only taking out a policy when you know the contract's terms and conditions well enough to set them to music.
c. Once you have started, always keeping it up. Life companies make most profit from those who withdraw early. Don't deny yourself the pleasure of ultimate satisfaction.

Friendly Societies

These are small, chummy versions of life insurance companies, with rudimentary record-keeping, door-to-door salesmen and pre-computer technology such as clipboards. Like life companies, they insure you against both death and sickness, and they invest your savings, but generally they charge you more. This is because much of your money is spent collecting small premiums and trying to work out what they were paid last year.

You can improve your position by:

a. Understanding the charging structure.
b. Comparing with other products.
c. Challenging their record-keeping.
d. Being persistent when the time comes for your payout (they may have lost all record of you).

Building Societies

There are real and pseudo building societies. The real ones are **mutual**, collective organisations, like the seven dwarfs. Even after the invasion of the carpet-baggers, they can be sleepy and dopey; they are unduly bashful about offering better mortgages and deposit rates than banks, and although happy and friendly most of the time, staff tend to be grumpy on Saturday mornings. However, the chill winds of competition have made them sneezy, an ailment for which company doctors prescribe modernisation.

Pseudos are like Red Riding Hood's wolf. Once real building societies, they have converted into banks. But they still hide behind that friendly, grandmotherly image, despite being big, ruthless, profit-centred, and, like most converts, pushy.

You can improve your position by:

a. Having a number of accounts. If one society converts to a pseudo you may net a windfall.
b. Going offshore (*q.v.*). Most building societies have Channel Islands branches which pay interest gross and at a higher rate.
c. Watching interest rates. Like buildings, they collapse faster than they rise.

National Savings

The government is not a big spender, it is a colossal spender. Every year it creates new taxes to finance its shopping, but they are always insufficient. It needs to borrow.

National Savings has the job of collecting money from the public and lending it to the government. There are branches hiding in Post Offices everywhere.

You can improve your position by:

Remembering that National Savings exists. Financial advisers won't prompt you because the government doesn't pay them commission.

Offshore

Anywhere other than the country you live in can be deemed to be 'offshore', but bluffers should restrict themselves to the financial meaning – a tax haven. Because of the imprecision, you can't look up an 'offshore fund' any more than you can find 'abroad' in the atlas: it isn't a location, more a fiscal attitude.

To sound streetwise, remember:

- The names of a few key tax havens – Bermuda, Guernsey and the Caymans are adequate for most purposes.
- Most offshore funds are still taxable, though tax is often payable later than with an onshore product.
- If anything goes wrong, you may have inadequate protection, as with driving off-road or skiing off-piste.

You can improve your position by:

Using offshore accounts appropriately. There's no reason to pay tax any sooner than the law requires.

BORROWING

We recommend rejecting the traditional maxim, 'Never a borrower or a lender be'. You *should* borrow money, when:

1. The interest on the loan is less than the profit you'll make by investing it. If you borrow £100,000, buy a piece of land and build a house on it, and then sell it for £250,000, borrowing was a smart move. The technical phrase to use here is **gearing**. So don't say, "I'm in debt up to my neck" but "I'm very highly geared".

2. You are temporarily out of money but still have basic needs. It is normal to seek to stay alive, and mature to acknowledge you only live once and want to enjoy it while it lasts. In this situation, borrowing should be called **managing your cashflow**. Rather than "I'm overdrawn again", say, "I'm experiencing a cashflow shortfall".

Overdrafts

Overdrafts are a particularly lucrative form of lending, because they involve:

- charging you interest on the overdraft;
- slapping a penalty on your account because 'you were warned';
- bouncing your cheques and charging you when they hit the ground;
- writing to say your account is in the red, and billing you for the letter.

This combination of interest and charges usually succeeds in absorbing any money you paid into the account to cover the original shortfall.

11

Unless you're a masochist, overdrafts should either be avoided, or converted into something more consensual. For instance:

1. Negotiate before you act. Banks treat you more gently when the overdraft has been agreed, or **authorised**, up front. The interest rate will be less, and you avoid nasty surprises.

2. Convert your overdraft into a loan with lower interest rates. But check for lock-in clauses which make early repayment expensive, and for penalties if you miss a repayment.

3. Move to a bank offering free overdrafts. In case this is a short-term gimmick, ask your bank manager to tell you if the rules change. Then he is on the hook, not you.

Personal Loans

Loans are like affairs. Some are brief, but useful in tiding you over a difficult period. Others are endless and drain all your resources. The secret is to know one from the other, before you get involved. Good bluffers:

1. Read all the paperwork. If you're confused, simply say you won't sign the form until you understand it. That will worry the financial adviser, who is probably as puzzled as you are. If he can unravel it, send his explanation to the company. Then (a) ask if he's correct, and (b) suggest they use his words to rewrite the form in plain English.

2. Refuse to be bulldozed even if the adviser says it is a 'limited offer', the rate is going up tomorrow and he'll be on holiday from Wednesday.

3. Keep a copy of the agreement and any correspondence. One day you may need to prove your point.

4. Remember that all loans have a **cooling off period**. This allows you to cancel the deal within a fixed time without suffering any penalty. It is a built-in safeguard against over-heated selling techniques.

When reading through the paperwork, look out for:

- The **term** of the loan. Some are for a fixed period, say five years. Others are open-ended. They may even have a half-term recess when you can choose whether to continue or quit.
- Any **penalties**. Like teachers, lenders may unexpectedly punish both harmless actions, like being a day late by mistake, and sensible ones, such as repaying a loan early.
- How the **interest is calculated**. The agreement should show the **APR** (see Glossary). For loans this is generally the true interest, and you should concentrate on this rather than what may be advertised as the 'headline' rate. If you are in any doubt, ask the financial adviser to add up how much you will pay overall. After all, he's got a calculator with compound interest buttons.
- The **repayment method**. Some require a lump sum at the end of the term, others monthly or yearly amounts.
- Conditions attached to any **discounts**. For example, will you have to give them back if you miss a monthly payment?
- The **security** the lender requires. If you fail to pay, will he seize your car, your house, or your CD collection? This also applies if you **guarantee** someone else's loan. Do you love him enough to put your shirt on the line? You might lose it.

Only the best financial advisers ask you the most critical question: how are you going to repay? This is particularly important when the money has been swapped for something that can't be sold, like clothes or a holiday. It also matters if you are buying an asset which reduces in value, like a new car.

At some point you will have to pay back the full sum you have borrowed – plus all the interest. If you can't, you're unlikely to be able to bluff your way past the bailiffs and the bankruptcy courts. Instead, shop at Oxfam and cycle to work – until you can afford your dream lifestyle.

Mortgages

A mortgage, like getting married and having a baby, is often misinterpreted as a sign of maturity. By the time you are 30, everyone expects you to have borrowed several times your annual income to buy a part-share in a terraced villa.

The best response is never to admit you 'can't afford' or 'don't want' a mortgage. This only inflames the situation. Instead, select from the following according to your audience:

– I'm expecting to inherit Uncle's Scottish estate.
– Of course your preoccupation with ownership is almost uniquely British. In Paris/Rome/New York everyone rents.
– I'm afraid my lover wouldn't hear of it.
– My Romany blood makes it difficult to settle in one place.

Obtaining a mortgage is like trekking in Afghanistan: it is an unregulated area, and the inhabitants hoodwink the unwary. If you are visiting for the first time, you may receive special treatment.

Usually this is more indulgent than that given to the regular traveller, involving cheap interest rates, larger discounts or substantial cashbacks. This generosity is designed to throw you off your guard, but we advise **first time buyers** to be no less vigilant than anyone else.

The following precautions are recommended by the Home Office*:

1. Carry identification. One point to sharpen and put under your belt is that you are the **mortgagor**, and the company is the **mortgagee**. Since grantors give to grantees, and employers to employees, this sounds as if it is the wrong way round – we talk about 'being given a mortgage'. But legally you have given the company a mortgage on your property, in exchange for a loan. The words mortgagor and mortgagee are a bluffer's delight: used correctly, they are a simple but definitive signal of your expertise.

2. Study the terrain. There are thousands of different mortgages. Shop around, talk to different providers, and if you are on the web, check the internet.

3. Time the journey. Most mortgages are for 25 years, but you can plea bargain for a shorter sentence, for instance if you are nearing retirement or hoping to get rich quick.

4. Decide your route. There are three main types of mortgage:

*Do not confuse with the Government Department of the same name run by the Home Secretary. Most homes run themselves these days, helped by a dishwasher, microwave and colour TV, and have no need of a secretary.

Interest only – You pay only the interest and have to find some way of paying back the capital at the end. Good if you are expecting to win the pools.

Repayment – The monthly payments are calculated to ensure that at the end of the mortgage period you will have paid back all the interest and all the capital.

Endowment (*q.v.*) – Each month you pay (a) your mortgage interest to the lender and (b) the premium on your endowment to the life insurance company. The endowment will pay out when you need to return the capital you borrowed, and hopefully at least the same amount. If it produces less, you could be in trouble. NB: If you are forced to take out an endowment with your lender, or your lender's best friend, ask about the commission they intend to take. You may shame them into sharing it.

5. Get vaccinated. There are many special mortgage deals, but the majority are short-term. After the honeymoon period, the monthly payments suddenly increase, causing 'payment shock'. It is better to inoculate yourself before you start out, by fully understanding the options:

Variable – This is the normal market rate, to which most tempting offers revert. Not all lenders charge the same variable rate, so compare your company with other lenders – if its rate is higher now, it will probably be equally excessive at the end of your special deal.

Discount – The mortgage is unnaturally cheap at the beginning, say for two to five years. But this discount may be paid for later by a higher variable rate. You may also be unable to move to a cheaper lender because the mortgage agreement has locked you in for a further period. Discounts can be disconcertingly expensive.

Fixed rate – The mortgage rate is fixed for a period, after which it reverts to the variable rate. But although the APR should show the interest rate you will pay over the whole term of the loan, fixed rate mortgages may craftily calculate it as if the lower rate applied for the whole period, so don't be caught out. And as with discounts, you may pay for the early lower rate with higher interest later in the mortgage, plus a lock-in period to stop you escaping to another lender.

Caps – These stop the rate moving above a predetermined point. For example, the mortgage may be capped at 9% for 5 years. So even if the market rate goes up to 15%, you will not pay more than 9%. Check for hidden costs and lock-ins.

Collars – Some mortgages have a minimum rate below which the interest cannot drop. Note that collars protect the lender's neck, not yours.

Cashback – The lender gives you a lump sum when you take out the mortgage. It can be useful for the unexpected costs of moving house, like eliminating dry rot or rodents.

6. Expect to be mugged. At some point in the journey you will be asked for more cash. Apart from legal fees and removal costs, common demands include:

Survey fees – The survey proves to the mortgage company that your house is worth at least what you're borrowing. Hint: If you want be able to sue a surveyor, you need a separate survey. Being paid twice helps cover their negligence claims.

Loan guarantee fee – Many special mortgage deals require you to pay a fee to 'earmark' the cash for your purchase. Check if this is refundable if you can't proceed – your best friend may gazump you and buy the house himself.

Administration costs – Charged by the lender for processing your application.

Compulsory insurance – This is like being forced to buy your potatoes at Harrods. Ask why, if the insurance is fairly priced, they have made it compulsory.

Mortgage indemnity guarantee – You should refer to this as a **MIG**, and always try to shoot it down. If your loan is for more than a certain percentage of the property's value, a MIG insures the lender against the house falling in value. It doesn't, however, insure you. What is worse is that some lenders also charge more interest because of the extra risk involved in a high percentage loan, so you are paying twice over. The final bombshell is that a MIG is not transferable. If you move house and transfer your mortgage, even with the same lender, you have to pay another MIG.

7. Know the worst. If you fail to keep up your mortgage payments, your house can be repossessed. This is frightening: banks are even tougher to exorcise than ghosts. If the nightmare does become reality, it is better to talk to your lender than simply send back the keys. You may be able to negotiate different terms – an extension of the loan period, or a 'payment holiday' because of unexpected redundancy. If the lender does reach the end of his tether, it is better if you do sell the house rather than

leaving it empty for the lender to put on the market. You will almost certainly get a better price.

However, selling isn't the end of the story. If the house fetches less than you borrowed, i.e. you have **negative equity**, the company will still pursue you for the excess. Hell hath no fury like a jilted lender.

8. Customise your exit. You can always change your lender, subject to lock-ins and other restrictions. But there are a number of traps which skilful bluffers side-step:

- Your new lender will charge you most of the items listed under (7). You should balance these costs against the benefits of the deal.

- If you are ever unemployed, the new mortgage may affect your entitlement to state support.

- You have a payment record with the old lender, so he may be more patient if you fall behind with your payments. This is the well known 'Better the devil you know than the devil you don't' principle of dealing with the financially big and powerful.

If you inherit some money, are paid a huge bonus, or write a bestseller, you can pay off your mortgage early – small print permitting. If you only pay off part of the capital, watch out. Interest is commonly calculated on mortgage debt once a year, say 31st December. A repayment on 2nd January is thus a 363 day interest-free loan to the lender. If you are inadvertently caught out by this underhand ploy, try suggesting that the company reciprocates, by lending you an equivalent amount of cash, interest free for the following year. They may be shamed into submission.

Credit Cards

If you have a piece of rope, you can make a ladder, tow your car home, or hang yourself. Credit cards are equally flexible.

It makes sense to:

a) Exploit the maximum interest-free credit period while saving your cash in a high interest account.
b) Select cards with no annual charge. Many give you the first year free. If they won't continue for the second, move elsewhere. You owe money, not loyalty.
c) Pay by direct debit, then you can blame the bank if the bill is settled late.

But beware of the noose: it's amazingly easy to acquire a wallet full of cards – particularly store cards. Their overuse stores up trouble, on which very high interest is payable. In fact most credit cards charge interest several times the normal borrowing rate. When banks lend at 8%, credit cards commonly demand 24%. This is as close to theft as anyone can get without being locked up.

Gold cards

If you haven't got a gold card, say that like Groucho Marx you spurn any club that would have you as a member. You can thus imply that gold cards are debased, like university degrees.

But privately acknowledge their uses. If you arrive in a strange town after dark, scruffy, wet and pushing a punctured bicycle, and the only hotel has five stars, a gold card allows you to bluff your way past the receptionist and reach the jacuzzi.

PROTECTING

Even people with the insurance equivalent of a bullet-proof vest have some exposed parts. Some think that 'protecting their assets' involves a jock strap, others may believe they have no assets worth insuring. Bluffers will advise these vulnerable souls that:

- Everyone owns at least one valuable possession – life itself, though this may be hard to accept on a wet Monday in Morecambe.
- Most people are capable of work, and its loss can be costly. One should never confuse capacity with motivation.
- It is usually cheaper to protect than replace your assets. But not always. Don't bother insuring your stereo if you live in a barge, bender, tree-house or student squat.

Self Protection

Life Assurance

Most insurance polices replace what you have lost. Life assurance* is the exception.

When your life insurance pays out, you won't benefit, because you'll be dead. This is brutal but true. Taking out a policy is an altruistic act which:

1. Pays off debts, such as a mortgage, so your family don't have to move into a tent when you die;

2. Gives money to dependants. You can thus threaten to cut them off without a penny, even though you haven't a cent to your name.

* It is classier to talk about life assurance than insurance. This shows you can distinguish the certainty of death from the risks of life.

Illness

Just as diseases arrive in various confusing forms, so does insurance against them. You will impress most consultants if you can distinguish between (a) medical insurance, (b) critical illness and (c) permanent health. Diagnostic tips include:

a. **Medical insurance** which pays private hospital bills if you are sick. But some common ailments, like toothache or problems in pregnancy, are regarded as self-inflicted and don't count.

b. **Permanent health** which pays you an income if you are off work because of sickness. Some policies pay out if you cannot do the job for which you are qualified, but others only cough up if you are unable to work at all.

c. **Critical illness** which pays a lump sum if you contract a serious illness. But it has to be so deadly serious that you are either almost extinct or totally disabled. For example, merely going blind is not enough – to get a payout, you have to be 100% blind in both eyes.

Accident

If your body is damaged by accident rather than disease, you need to claim under a personal accident policy. This contains a gruesome list of severable body parts, rather like a self-assembly kit in reverse. It then excludes all the most likely methods of misplacing them, such as skiing and riding a motor bike. Living dangerously costs extra premiums.

You can also insure any body part against damage or accident. Pianists may insure their fingers, footballers their feet. However insurance may be refused for prostitutes, as their profession remains officially unacceptable (on grounds of public policy), despite being underwritten by councillors, MPs and members of the judiciary.

Possessions Protection

This is like an exam syllabus with three compulsory sections: **home**, **contents** and **car**, and two options: **personal possessions** (losing things outside the home) and **accidental damage** (you manage to break a window without a burglar's help).

You can ignore the options and hope the topic never comes up. If you don't cover the compulsory sections, you are taking a bigger risk.

When revising your insurance, consider:

- Other providers. You may get cheaper cover elsewhere. But don't forget to review their results record. It's no good paying less for the premium if the new company quibbles over every claim.
- What you've overlooked. Some things are so much part of the furniture, you don't notice them until they're stolen.
- Bonuses. If a claim would substantially increase next year's premiums, it may be cheaper to repair the roof yourself.
- New for old. This allows you to replace your stolen video without spending a year debating its second-hand value.
- Excess. You agree to cover the first part of every claim, making the premium marginally less excessive.
- Subsidence. If your house is likely to go through the floor, the cost goes through the roof.
- Postcodes. Some areas are prohibitively expensive, others uninsurable. In these cases, insurance is not the answer. Consider moving.

Income Protection

This gives you an income if you become unemployed, though you are disqualified if you:

- resign
- retire
- take voluntary redundancy
- are fired because of a 'wilful act' on your part, such as being uncivil to your boss.

Debt Protection

Even those with negative assets need insurance. If you (a) owe money, and (b) become unemployed, have an accident, get sick or die, you may be unable to pay back what you borrowed. This could add bankruptcy to your 'never rains but it pours' scenario.

Loan protection insurance pays off the debts for you. Alternatives are:

1. Using savings to pay off the loan.
2. Selling your collection of 1960s comics to raise money.
3. Emigrating to Brazil.

SAVING

Just as Caesar dreamt of world conquest, and Einstein yearned to understand relativity, so today's visionaries lie awake at night designing the perfect savings **product**. This paragon will display the following characteristics, called **key features** by financial advisers (or agents):

- High returns: lots of money back in return for a small investment. The lottery is a good example.

- Low risk: you never lose the money you invest. The lottery is a bad example.

- No tax: therefore no compulsory profit-sharing with the government.

- Invisible (and outrageous) charges. They make a fortune and you don't notice.

Currently, the financial institutions compete in the savings supermarket. As you hover at the door wondering which aisle to browse, a salesman will appear. For a share of your spending money, he will help with your shopping.

It is reasonable to ask at this point why you should need a paid guide to select an investment product when you are perfectly capable of picking your way through 35 varieties of yoghurt and 16 different binliners. A plausible answer is that it is easy to be baffled by the language of savings. It's like seeing shelves full of salad dressings, but not knowing which is low calorie because all the labels are in Latin.

But just as there are only a few reasons for choosing one mayonnaise over another, so there are only a handful of factors which distinguish savings products. These are **T**axbusting, **R**isk of rip-offs, **A**ccessibility,

25

Capital security and the Klondike. Measuring a product against these five tests allows the bluffer to know if it is on **TRACK**. This list shows what a high score in each category means:

Taxbusting: You trounce the taxman.
Risk of rip-offs: Definite daylight robbery.
Access: You choose when to retrieve your money.
Capital security: Your original investment is as safe as houses.
Klondike: You've bought a gold mine.

Current Accounts

These are money management mechanisms rather than saving devices. Cash runs through the account like electricity, brightening up your life but also capable of nasty shocks.

Taxbusting: 0%. Unless you are a non-taxpayer, when you can fill in a form and get it paid gross.
Risk of rip-offs: 15%. Check for charges, overdrafts, withdrawal conditions.
Access: 100%. Most have cashpoints; some allow 24 hour telephone access, ideal for insomniacs.
Capital security: 99%. The slight erosion caused by inflation is eliminated if you spend the cash quickly.
Klondike: 0.5%. Some pay interest, but mostly at low rates. Finding the exceptions may be worth the hassle of moving all your direct debits.

Deposit Accounts

These are the sliced bread of the financial supermarket, available at all banks, building societies, and some insurance companies. You lend them your money and they pay you interest. When comparing rates between providers, remember to use the full **Compounded Annual Rate** (**CAR**) as this takes into account the frequency of interest payments. The advertised headline rate may drive your real returns into the ditch.

Taxbusting: 0%. As for current accounts.
Risk of rip-offs: 10%. Regular surveillance required in case the rate is sneakily reduced.
Access: 100%. But some have notice periods. You pay a penalty if you withdraw money without noticing them.
Capital security: 95%. Over time inflation erodes your capital value.
Klondike: 2%. Gold diggers should move elsewhere.

Endowments

These are sold by insurance companies. You give them your money for at least 10 years, and they invest it, mostly on the stockmarket.

Taxbusting: -50% to 50%. Basic rate tax is paid on your behalf by the company, whether you are a taxpayer or not. No higher rate tax is due. So it's taxbusting for the wealthy; taxpunitive for the poor.
Risk of rip-offs: 35%. Check the small print for penalties and charges.
Access: 25%. Endowments are linked to a life insurance policy so your relatives and friends get a windfall if you die. Otherwise trying to escape from an endowment makes divorce look cheap.
Capital security: 95%. If you die, or survive and continue paying until the end of the term, you have a guaranteed **sum assured**.
Klondike: 15%. You receive annual bonuses, plus a final **terminal** bonus. If the stockmarket has done

well the bonuses should reflect this. If they don't, ask if the actuaries have made an error in the generation game, by either (a) releasing too much in the past, so you lose out to earlier generations of policyholders, or (b) hiding too much in their back pockets for future members. If so, claim mistaken identity: some of this money should be identified as yours.

Life Annuities

An annuity is a gamble on your own life, like Russian roulette. You give a lump sum to an insurance company, and they pay you a sum every month for the rest of your life. If you survive longer than expected, your winnings are effectively paid by those who passed away early. It's a grisly subsidy, but it works.

Before you gamble, check the terms. There are a wide range of annuity rates, so review the providers before deciding which casino to patronise.

Taxbusting: up to 60%. A percentage of each monthly payment is tax-free, because it is treated as a return of the capital with which you bought the annuity. If you live longer than anticipated, the tax-free payments continue even though you have had all your capital back. Survivors thus have the double pleasure of defeating both Death and the Taxman.

Risk of rip-offs: 30%. The Casino never loses.

Access: 0%. It's a life sentence.

Capital security: 0%. They keep your money. More costly variants return some cash to your relatives if you die very quickly. But it may be unhealthy to broadcast this.

Klondike: 25%. If you live longer than average, you do well. The undead make a killing.

Shares

This is the ultimate DIY investment product. Instead of lending your money to a financial institution and letting them decide what to buy, you choose. You receive regular dividends and make gains or losses when you sell.

Taxbusting: 20%. Income tax is payable on dividends; profits are subject to capital gains tax (CGT). You may be able use reliefs and exemptions to shelter from CGT.

Risk of rip-offs: 20%. Fees to brokers, stamp duty to the government, plus dealing spreads – the intermediary who buys or sells your shares always takes a cut.

Access: 90%. You can sell whenever the markets are open. But if you need money in a hurry your shares might be depressed, spoiling your profits and your mood.

Capital security: -10%. You can lose all your money and pay dealing costs on top.

Klondike: 100%. Unlimited upside. The gold digging secret is:

> **d**iscover undervalued companies;
> **i**nvest;
> **g**ossip, so demand pushes up the price; then
> **s**ell at a profit.

Unit Trusts

These are sold by fund management and insurance companies. Instead of buying shares, corporate bonds or property directly, you buy units in a fund. The fund then buys the assets and splits the profits or losses between unit-holders.

Taxbusting: 30%. You pay income tax on any dividends, plus capital gains tax on any profits when you sell the units. The fund itself can buy and sell shares without paying CGT, and so acts as a tax deferral mechanism.

Risk of rip-offs: 45%. Units are sold at one price and bought at another: this is called the spread. You always lose and the manager always wins. In addition there are numerous charges – entry, exit, annual, and special.

Access: 90%. You can buy and sell at any time the market is open, but if you want your money quickly you may be forced to sell when the markets are weak, and your units cheap.

Capital security: 0%. You could lose all your capital, though this is less likely than if you invested in the assets directly. The fund should spread its risk to protect you.

Klondike: 90%. You might uncover a gem.

Investment Trusts

Similar to a unit trust, but instead of units you buy shares in a company. It then uses your investment to buy shares and bonds in the stock market.

For all practical purposes, score as for unit trusts. The only real difference is that you pay some of your rip-off charges to the broker who buys and sells the shares for you, rather than to the manager of the unit trust. This is unlikely to make you feel any better.

Open Ended Investment Companies

A European import, **OEICs** are expected to replace both unit and investment trusts. Again, score as for unit trusts. Although there is no bid/offer spread, ingenious fund managers can still coax plenty of money out of your fund.

OEICs (pronounced OIKS) are still regarded with distrust, so when you talk about them, leave the context sufficiently vague so no-one is quite sure whether you are referring to the agent, the company or the product.

Individual Savings Accounts (ISAs)

These are a tax wrapper around a collection of investments such as life insurance, deposit accounts, cash, equities, corporate bonds, unit and investment trusts and OEICs.

Taxbusting: 100%. Free of income tax and CGT.
Risk of rip-offs: 20%. Read the small print, especially for more complex products.
Access: 85%. You should be able to withdraw funds from the ISA, but individual ISA managers may make this difficult or expensive.
Capital security: ?%. Depends very much what is inside the ISA – the super-performing shares of the century (100%), bank deposits (3%) or speculative SE Asian failures (-10%).
Klondike: ?%. From 0-100%, depending on the wrapper's contents.

TESSAs

Tessa's full name is **Tax Exempt Special Savings Account**, and she inhabits most banks and building societies. You are allowed to save up to £9,000 in your first TESSA over a five year period. If you began the relationship early enough, you may be able to roll her over and start again.

Taxbusting: 100%. No income tax, providing you keep the interest in the TESSA for the full period.

Risk of rip-offs: 7%. Some providers entice with high interest rates, then cut them severely once you're inside.

Access: 80%. You can withdraw, but it destroys the tax-efficiency.

Capital security: 95%. Inflation gradually shrinks the capital value.

Klondike: 8%. More interesting than most deposit accounts.

PEPs

PEP is a nickname for **Personal Equity Plan**. It is a tax wrapper around corporate bonds, shares, unit or investment trusts.

Taxbusting: 100%. No income tax or CGT.

Risk of rip-offs: 40%. PEP charges may wipe out the tax saving for all except higher rate taxpayers.

Access: 85%. You can wrap it up at any time, but your provider may impose exit charges.

Capital security: ?%. Depends on what you hold inside the PEP – you can lose everything.

Klondike: 99%. You could strike gold.

Bonds

These come in so many versions that some bluffers believe it is enough to know only that 'The name is Bond'. But if you want to see your agent shaken, if not stirred, there is no substitute for cracking the numerical code.

001: UK Government Bonds

Also known as **gilts**. You lend your money to the government and it pays you interest at a fixed rate. Each gilt has a date when it **matures** (is repaid).

You can unsettle most financial advisers by asking why they don't recommend gilts as an investment, and whether their opinion would change if the government paid commission.

Taxbusting: 35%. The interest is taxable, but any profit on sale is free from capital gains tax. Gilts have also been exempt from stamp duty since 1804 – dropping this little fact into conversation does wonders for your credibility.

Risk of rip-offs: 2%. Fees when you buy and sell.

Access: 98%. You don't have to wait until the gilt matures. You can sell it (a) via a stockbroker or (b) at the post office, if you have the patience to queue.

Capital security: 90%. Even anarchists can afford to ignore the risk that the government won't pay them back. A bigger danger is a fall in the market value because either (a) interest rates generally fall (making the rate on your bond relatively more attractive), or (b) the pound becomes stronger (making the bond worth more to people overseas). Inflation can also eat into returns, although some gilts are protected by **index-linking**.

Klondike: 7%. Better interest rates than banks. Plus if the market value goes up, you can sell your bond at a profit.

002: Corporate Bonds

A company borrows money, usually from financial institutions (*q.v.*), and gives them a certificate or IOU. Some of these IOUs can be split up and sold in bite-sized pieces to the public.

Taxbusting: 35%. The interest is taxable, but there is no stamp duty. Any profit on sale is free of Capital Gains Tax. Unfortunately, this also means losses are useless.

Risk of rip-offs: 3%. Fees to stockbrokers for buying and selling the bonds.

Access: 98%. If you don't want to wait until maturity, you can sell your adolescent bonds via a stockbroker.

Capital security: 85%. Either the company could go bust, or the value of the bond could drop. However some bonds pay **floating** interest rates, which stay at market levels and protect your capital value from sinking.

Klondike: 8%. Rewards depend on the company. Precarious businesses pay a higher interest rate. As with gilts, the bond's market value could rise, for instance if the currency of the bond strengthens or interest rates fall.

003: Single Premium Bonds

The principle of a single premium bond is simple: you give a lump sum to a financial institution for a fixed period, usually at least five years, and they give it back at the end. You hope there will be some profit or bonus as well.

This simplicity is, however, deceptive. No-one finds these bonds easy to understand, so it is not only acceptable but necessary to admit that they are confusing. This has two causes:

1. Single premium bonds used to be sold only by insurance companies, but now banks and building societies are issuing look-alikes. Insurance company single premium bonds have a unique ingredient – a

taxbusting potential – which may not be shared by the imitations.

2. The old-fashioned single premium bond has spawned two modern children, Guaranteed Income Bonds (004) and Guaranteed Equity Bonds (005). These may have some of the qualities of the single premium bond, but you can guarantee that they are even more complicated.

The best way of dealing with this choice is to review the ingredients and pick the ones you would like. Tax-free withdrawals and guaranteed income? Or stock-market links and your tax back at the end? There are so many combinations available that you can be almost certain of finding what you want. If you can't, apply for a job in the financial services industry and build your own.

The vital statistics of a vanilla-flavoured, insurance-company-issued single premium bond are:

Taxbusting: 40%. Too complicated even for some tax-men. It's worth grasping just to call their bluff:

- 5% can be paid to you every year tax-free because it is treated as a return of your original capital.
- This annual payment is officially a tax deferral, as the full profit (including 5% withdrawals) is taxable when you get the final payout.
- You can turn the tax deferral into permanent tax-saving if you stop being a higher rate tax-payer before the policy matures.
- If you move to a tax haven the payout is tax free.

A word of warning: these steps don't work if you are a non-taxpayer. Basic rate tax is paid by the company and you can't get it back. So these bonds are a treacherous tax-trap for non-taxpayers.

Risk of rip-offs: 30%. Check the paperwork carefully for charges and penalties. If you find any you haven't been warned about, give your adviser a free kick.

Access: 30%. You can recover your money, but if you do this too quickly you'll lose part of your capital in charges. The sooner you change your mind, the worse it is. Women receive no special privileges from this bond.

Capital security: 75%. The capital is not normally guaranteed, but if you hold for (say) five years it is rare for you to get back less than you paid in.

Klondike: 12%. There is no fixed return, but if the company does well you get a share. But then so do the directors and shareholders, so don't get too excited.

004: Guaranteed Income Bonds

You should always refer to these as **GIBs**. They are sold mostly by insurance companies, but also by banks and building societies. You lend them your money and they pay you a guaranteed interest rate for a fixed period.

Taxbusting: ?%. Depends whether it is, at heart, a single premium bond (*q.v.*). If so, the tax treatment is the same. Otherwise it is taxed at your top rate when you get the payout.

Risk of rip-offs: 50%. Read the small print carefully, and then read it again. Turn the product inside out and check the lining.

Access: 5%. Generally your money can only be accessed at the end of the period, unless you adopt extreme tactics, such as dying.

Capital security: 85%. Most guarantee to return

your capital, but check the small print. They may only guarantee the interest and use the capital to pay it: a devious trick.

Klondike: 6%. Ask if the interest payments are before or after tax (no prizes for guessing which is more common), and whether the headline rate is paid throughout, or drops after the first year. Beware of rates which are 'linked' to the base rate. Meths is also linked to champagne.

005: Guaranteed Equity Bonds

GEBs are sold mostly by insurance companies but also by other financial institutions. You lend your money to the company and they invest it on the stock-market for a fixed period.

Make it clear up-front that you know that 'guaranteed equity' has nothing to do with promising to be fair. Indeed, it is sometimes worryingly unclear what is being guaranteed, other than the agent's commission and the company's charges.

Taxbusting: -10%. Unless this is a single premium bond (*q.v.*) the final payout is taxable as income, even though most of it was a capital gain.

Risk of rip-offs: 60%. Lots of opportunity for inventive complicated conditions.

Access: 10%. Heavy penalties if you want your money back early.

Capital security: 60%. Read the paperwork carefully. Some bonds are fully guaranteed, some only seem to be.

Klondike: 40%. If the market does well, this will be reflected in your returns. But your upside will be capped – the company keeps part of the profits.

006: National Savings Bonds

These are sold by the UK government via Post Offices. You lend your money to the State for a fixed period and it pays you interest.

Taxbusting: 0-100%. Some bonds are taxable, some tax-free.
Risk of rip-offs: 0%. Straightforward.
Access: 75%. Bonds are usually for 5 years. Early withdrawal is possible but you lose substantial interest.
Capital security: 95%+. Fixed rate bonds are eroded by inflation; index-linked bonds cover inflation plus a small profit.
Klondike: 5-8%. Usually better than deposit accounts, especially to higher rate taxpayers.

007: Premium Bonds

Sold by National Savings. You lend the government your money and they put your numbers in a prize draw every month.

Taxbusting: 100%. Prizes are tax-free
Risk of rip-offs: 1%. You can't win in the first month.
Access: 100%. Bonds are repayable on demand.
Capital security: 95%. Your capital is returned but inflation will erode it.
Klondike: 100%. You could become a millionaire.

THE PENSIONS PALACE

People put off thinking about paunches and pensions for the same reason: a perfectly understandable belief in eternal youth. But, unless you're Peter Pan, even the best bluffers grow old. Better to remind others of a fairy story...

Once upon a time there was a wonderful palace. Advertisements fluttered from its battlements and surpluses stockpiled in its storerooms. Inside the palace lived hundreds of beautiful pensions. Not that they were seen by ordinary people, of course. The common folk only met the knights who lived in the castle.

"Give us a share of your earnings every month," the knights suggested. "Then, when you are too old to work, we will give you a beautiful pension. She will stay with you and care for you for the rest of your life".

It was an irresistible offer. The people began paying the knights every month and every evening they fell asleep dreaming of the beautiful pension which would one day be theirs.

But inside the castle all was not as it seemed. The tower where the pensions lived was guarded by two old and sleepy soldiers, called Compliance and After-the-Event. The knights found it easy to charge past them and steal whatever they wanted.

No-one protected the pensions properly. Not the actuaries, who lived in the North Tower and stored up provisions, not the owners of the palace who lived far away and rarely visited, nor the princes who hung out in the billiard room.

Every year the princes met to decide the same question: should they hunt short-term profits (for the owners) or long-term returns (for the pensions)? And every year their answer was the same. This wasn't surprising, as their salary and bonus were linked to short-term profits, and by the time anyone saw a long-term return the princes would all have moved on to other palaces.

And so it went on for many years. Then one day there was a loud knocking at the palace door. It was the oldest man in the village. "I'm too old to work any more," he said. "I've come for my pension". But the princes sent some actuaries to talk to him, and he went away bewildered. Then a second and a third visitor came, all asking for their pensions. But the knights persuaded them to take away with them, not a beautiful pension, but her sisters Wormwood and Wizened...

If you want a happy ending, you must bluff your way past the knights and find out what is really happening in the palace. To succeed you need inside information, such as knowing that pensions are split between a **state** room, an **occupational** room and the much abused **personal** room. Between each are doors, tunnels and secret passages, and they all contain both booby traps and a gateway into the annex or **retiring** room. You need to know what is in each room, how to move from one room to the next, and when and how to enter the annex.

State Pensions

In order to receive the basic state pension, you must have paid National Insurance Contributions for most of your working life. If you are not sure whether you qualify, or don't know how small your pension will be, write and ask the Contributions Agency at Longbenton in Newcastle. Finding out long before you retire gives you the maximum opportunity to clear up any misunderstandings.

National Insurance Contributions are a skilful bluff. It is commonly believed that 'Contributions' are paid in to your future pension, but in reality the money is a tax used for motorways, missiles and the prime minister's parties. To show you are an insider, always refer to a National Insurance Contribution by its abbreviation, **NIC**.

The most frequent question ever asked about NICs is, "Are you contracted in or contracted out?" Resist any temptation to talk about bridge games or gangsters. In the world of pensions the expressions 'contract in' or 'contract out' have only one context – the State Earnings Related Pensions Scheme, which everyone calls **SERPS**.

SERPS was a bold attempt to link the basic state pension to employees' earnings. But it quickly became so expensive that the government started both shrinking its value and bribing people to leave it. These pay-offs, officially called **rebates**, are paid into the individual's own pension fund – either occupational or personal. If you haven't got either, you can still contract out, but the pension company may levy punitive charges. Don't try and contract out if you are self-employed, because SERPS never covered you in the first place.

And never assume you can survive on a basic State Pension. If that is your only income, you will be below the official poverty line. To keep your head above water, you need:

1. A second pension: occupational, personal, SERPS or all three; or
2. A private income, for instance from investments, state benefits or home-grown whiz-kids; or
3. To go on working until you kick the bucket.

Occupational Pensions

These are set up by employers for their workers, and come in one of two varieties: final salary, and money purchase.

Final salary schemes guarantee to pay a pension based on your earnings just before retirement. The exact amount depends on how long you have worked for the company, and the rules of the scheme, but because of the calculation method, retiring early always takes a big bite out of a final salary pension.

Bluffers should know two key facts about final salary schemes:

1. They are the employer's problem. He has guaranteed to pay certain benefits related to your earnings, and if the pension fund is too small, he has to step in and top it up.

2. In practice there is almost no ceiling on what the employer can put into the fund for you. Increasing your influence over him is thus the single most effective way of improving your pension.

Money purchase schemes pay you a pension based on what has been collected in the pension fund. So if there's a shortfall, it's down to the employees. Some penny-pinching companies cut costs by moving from final salary to money purchase, and pretend it's to give you greater flexibility. Call their bluff and ask for the calculations behind the decision.

Both occupational and money purchase schemes can either be **contributory** or **non-contributory**. With a non-contributory scheme the employer pays and you don't need to contribute. In a contributory scheme you put a percentage of your salary into the fund together with the employer's contribution.

In either case you can volunteer to pay more, with an **additional voluntary contribution** (AVC).

Because of the tax relief on pensions, the Revenue have set limits on what you can contribute, in case you save too much and upset their cashflow. These limits are based on your earnings in a tax year. You can get an unexpected win by knowing that earnings for this purpose includes overtime, bonuses and benefits, such as your company car.

There is an alternative to the employer's AVC scheme, called a **FSAVC**. The FS officially stands for **Free Standing**, i.e. not linked to an employer's scheme, but 'False Substitute' might be more appropriate. This is because an FSAVC is no more an alternative for an AVC than cooking chocolate is for Belgian truffles. If anyone still recommends you move to an FSAVC, ask about the charges. FSAVCs with lower charges than AVCs qualify as endangered species.

If you have an occupational scheme and leave your job within two years, you can take out most of your money (but not your employer's). If you've served a longer sentence, you have a choice:

1. Transfer the fund to your new employer's occupational scheme;

2. Transfer it to a personal pension (*q.v.*);

3. Leave it. Your employer will then be obliged to pretend he gave you a pay rise each year and will calculate your pension accordingly. Expect this sham salary increase to be even lower than the pathetically small rise you would have got if you had stayed. After all, you lost your most effective bargaining counter by quitting.

If you ever argue with your employer about pensions, watch out for his verbal backhand. Keep up a sustained volley by lobbing in a few of the following:

- **Defined Contribution** means money purchase, and **defined benefit** means final salary. **COMPS** is short for **contracted-out money purchase scheme**.
- When there is too much money in a final salary scheme, the employer can take a **contribution holiday**. This over-funding is usually caused by freak market returns and is thus rarely well-earned, unlike your annual leave.
- A **deficit** is the opposite: there is insufficient money in the fund to meet its obligations.
- A **preserved pension** is left behind when you move to a new job. Like preserved fruit, it is rarely as good as the fresh variety, and can leave a sour taste. .
- An **earnings cap** may not fit, but the taxman forces you to wear it. It is a salary ceiling roughly equal to the highest wages in the Inland Revenue. Any amounts above this are ignored for pension contributions purposes.
- **Added years** is when the company pretends you've been employed for longer than you have, and gives you a bigger pension. In reality you've probably worked the extra years as overtime.

Personal Pensions

This is your own savings pot, out of which your pension will be paid. So the bigger the pot, the higher the pension. Again, the Revenue hover around like traffic wardens, making sure you don't park too much money in your scheme. They permit you a little more freedom with a personal pension than an occupational scheme, enough so you can **carry forward** and **carry back** various limits and entitlements, but not so much that you get carried away with excitement.

This flexibility is some small compensation for the fact that employers rarely contribute to a personal pension, so if you have the choice you should generally stay in your occupational scheme rather than **opting out** into a personal pension.

There was a time when agents persuaded thousands of people to transfer out of occupational schemes, raking off huge commissions in the process. You should refer to this **pensions misselling** as a fiasco, a debacle and a scandal, preferably all in the same sentence.

But misselling is not the only vice of which personal pensions stand accused. Another is **PUPs – Paid Up Pensions**. As the individual is the only contributor to most personal pensions, if you stop paying the premiums, the company may close the policy. But of course it goes on mining your fund for charges, and this can extract all your savings. So if you want to avoid a PUP, remember – a pension is for life, not just for Christmas.

Despite all this bad news, personal pensions have some advantages. For instance, to get a payout you don't actually have to stop work, you merely have to be at least 50 years old. So a small personal pension could ease you into retirement.

When selecting a personal pension, first check the charges, and then ask:

1. What's the fund's performance record? It may not be repeated in the future, but unless you are clairvoyant, it's the best evidence you've got.

2. Who chooses where my money goes? You may have your own ideas.

3. What happens if I get sick? Some schemes have a **waiver of premium** option, an insurance policy which pays your pension contributions if you are ill.

4. **What happens if I just want to take a break?** You need a scheme which allows **contribution holidays**.

If you are disillusioned with pension companies, try:

- Doing it yourself. But a **Self Invested Personal Pension** or **SIPP** merely gives a taste of independence. It allows you to select the assets in which your pension fund is invested, but you still have to pay professionals to manage it. This is because the government thinks you might spend it yourself before you retire. Occupational schemes are of course safe with employers – ask the Maxwell pensioners.
- Banding together. **Group personal pensions (GPPs)** should benefit from economies of scale and so charge you less. Some employers will pay the set-up costs of a GPP scheme, and use their extra muscle to negotiate on your behalf. But check that you can remain in the pension if you leave your job – you don't want to have been sold a pup.
- Opting for **single premiums** rather than **regular premiums**. Under a single premium contract you pay a lump sum for the whole year. Then next year you work out how much you want to contribute, and pay another single premium. This has many advantages:

    a) You have complete flexibility, so you can adjust your payments each year.
    b) The charges may be lower.
    c) You can pay into more than one scheme, which spreads your risks.
    d) You can backdate the single premium one year, so you know exactly how much you earned and what the taxman will allow you to contribute.

The disadvantages are down to you. Can you save the lump sum you need to contribute, without the discipline of a regular deduction? If you are bluffing at this point you're only kidding yourself.

Retirement

At this point you discover whether you have success-fully outmanoeuvred your pension provider. If you have, you have won a battle, but the bluffing isn't over yet.

The amount you receive from your **state** and **occupational** pensions depends on your contribution/employment record. The good news is that your pension increases every year; but the bad news is that the increase will be infinitesimal. This is because the basic state pension is linked to prices rather than earnings, so state pensioners' standard of living falls relative to those in work. Most occupational schemes are similar but worse, as they cap any increase to 5%. The technical term for this unpleasant device is **Limited Price Indexation**. It means the price you can afford to pay for anything becomes more limited as you get older.

A personal pension works differently. The sum you've saved is swapped for an annuity. This is a guarantee by the company paying the annuity that they will give you a fixed sum every month for the rest of your life. The key question is 'how much?'.

To decide this, the insurance company looks into its crystal ball and predicts:

a. how long they think you will live, and

b. which way interest rates will move over the rest of your life.

In practice they tend to be conservative – i.e. any errors are in their favour. They also look only a few years ahead. So if interest rates are expected to be low, you get a small income. If rates, prices and costs all rise, this small amount could shrink till it becomes invisible to the naked eye.

We recommend treating the onset of your annuity like the onset of puberty: planning ahead makes it less painful.

1. Beware of sudden stock market swings just before you take the annuity. An unexpected downturn could upset the performance of your fund, giving you a depressingly small lump sum. You may want to insulate your fund from this volatility, by moving it into something more stable, like gilts (*q.v.*) in the period just before you switch.

2. Take advantage of the **open market option**. This allows you to pick the company offering the best annuity. You don't have to stay with the financial institution which looked after the fund while it was growing. But some treat transfers as desertions and punish you accordingly. Check the terms before you start saving to make sure you are not joining the pensions equivalent of the French Foreign Legion.

3. Instead of a level annuity, which stays the same for ever, you can choose:
   - an escalator, rising each year;
   - an index-linked annuity, which keeps pace with inflation;
   - an annuity with a survivor's pension, to keep your lover in clover.

These bells and whistles make the annuity much more expensive – but they may be worth their weight in gold.

4. Consider **deferring** the annuity. If you don't need a pension immediately, you can leave your fund to grow. If you do this, annuity rates may improve, if only because you will be older.

5. Opt for **drawdown**. This allows you (a) to defer your pension, so the fund continues to grow, and (b) still take some cash out of the fund. In practice, unless you have a sizeable fund, the charges make drawdown a let down.

In general you cannot take a personal pension earlier than 50 or later than 75. But special rules apply to some short-lived professions. Downhill skiers can retire at 30, cyclists and tennis players at 35, along with models and wrestlers. Golfers, motorcyclists and trapeze artists all finish at 40. This is ironic, given that most desk-bound workers are hoping to spend their retirement skiing, playing golf and riding a Norton Commando across Colorado.

Note that both occupational and personal schemes allow you to take some of your pension as a tax-free lump sum, but that this is such sheer good news it is unlikely to last.

CHOOSING FINANCIAL ADVISERS

All financial advisers are intermediaries, or go-betweens, between you and the company which supplies the product. They can also be referred to as **agents**, although it is often unclear whether they are your agent or the company's. Establishing an agent's true loyalties, working out whose side he is really on, is one of the key problems of this sometimes murky world.

Another difficulty is the number of agencies and types of operator. Some agents are on one side, some on another, others are double agents or work independently. To clarify these muddy waters, the **Regulator** (known as 'R') has divided all UK operatives into two groups.

1. **Tied agents**, who are bound to a single company, and agree to sell only that company's products.

2. **Independent financial advisers**, or **IFAs** who are freelancers and must sell a range of products.

When they first meet a client, UK agents are obliged by law to identify themselves as either a tied agent or an IFA. But this requirement is useless unless you know the meaning of these calling cards.

Tied Agents

Tied agents cannot sell you a product made by a competitor. So if you already know you want a pension from Reliability Assurance Plc, their tied agent will explain the different pension policies sold by that company and discuss which would be best for you. But if you don't know which company's pension you want, he can't tell you.

There is a special sub-class of tied agents, selling what is known as **industrial business** (**IB**). This is a euphemism for door-to-door money collection, little different from buying lucky white heather.

The IB agent comes by every week or month and collects your money, marking it off in a little note-book. He is thus a handy substitute for social services in areas where the council no longer visit the elderly or disabled. This collection cost has to come out of the premiums which makes IB policies relatively expensive, but does relieve families of the need to visit granny quite so often.

Despite the oaths of loyalty taken by tied agents, some do cross the border and sign up with a rival out-fit. Some operatives even cross the iron curtain between IFAs and tied agents, and make a new life for themselves on the other side.

Independent Financial Advisers

IFAs make a living by selling the products of many providers. Some choose to specialise in an area, such as pensions, but they must still sell a range of different companies' products.

Many IFAs are paid on commission. So a product which pays 1% commission may not do as well in the market place as one which pays 6%. If you ask an IFA, of course, there will always be other differences between the two which make it entirely reasonable to choose the 6% product.

Other advisers are fee-based so you either rent by the hour, or pay a pre-agreed fixed cost. So you may give £400 for 4 hours work, at the end of which you have arranged a pension. Or the adviser may agree to help you find a pension, in exchange for £300 – whether it takes him or her an hour or a day.

Spotting a Good Agent

There are only two ways of finding a good agent, recommendation and interrogation.

Interrogation is the classic route. Ask for a preliminary half-hour discussion, which you should get for free – you are a bluffer, after all. During your cross-examination, notice whether:

- He recommends any product which pays no commission, such as gilts or National Savings bonds (*q.v.*). Award 20 points for each.

- He takes phone calls on his mobile during your meeting. If he does, deduct 15 points. A truly professional adviser will concentrate on you.

- He suggests you cancel a policy you took out recently and replace it with another. This is called 'churning' and is a quick way of skimming money into the adviser's pocket. He will get commission on the new policy and you will receive very little for the old. Comment that, with churning, the cream goes to fat cat salesmen, and deduct 40 points.

- He can meet your specific needs. Few agents are generalists, and if you want your financial identity restructured, ask whether he or his partners can deal with the whole picture. For instance, you may need some specialist tax advice – are the advisers qualified to give this, or merely able to explain the general tax consequences of certain products? If he can, add 35 points; if he recognises his limitations, add 15. Honesty is a better policy than some you will be offered. If he bluffs, deduct 20. That's your prerogative.

You need to find an adviser who scores at least 50 points. But even if you do, uncertainty always remains. A large part of every agent's work remains undercover for years. It may be three decades before your pension is activated, or a sudden death triggers an insurance policy. And it is only then that you really know whether your agent was truly what he seemed.

Best Advice

This is a good opportunity for you to show off, by exploding two commonly held assumptions:

1. That a good agent will provide good advice, and the best agent, should you ever locate him, the best advice. This is not the case. All advisers are required to provide so-called 'best advice'.

2. That 'best advice' means the adviser is required to sell you the product which best suits your needs. This is only true if he is an IFA. Tied agents are only obliged to tell you which of their company's products is the best for you. So it could be the worst life insurance policy on the market, but if you are buying from a tied agent and what you need is a life insurance policy, this will be 'best advice'. This is a classic case of word-bending. In the world of Financial Services, remember that you can often do much better than 'best'.

Fact Finds

Thorough research is an indispensable and time-consuming part of every financial adviser's job. Few travel agents, for instance, have customers who come in and say "I've got some time off. I'd like a holiday. Where shall I go?" But the same people will arrive at their financial advisers and announce, "I've got some money I'd like to invest. Where shall I put it?"

Before the adviser can answer, he has to do a 'Fact Find'. This is a lengthy questionnaire about your life, expectations, investments and available cash. Your answers are the foundation of the adviser's recommendations, which arrive arm in arm with illustrations, showing how much you will pay, for how long, for which product, for what return.

Illustrations should be tailored to your requirements, but, as with holiday brochures, watch out for conventional glosses. The brochure may show bronzed, bikini-clad beauties in a resort which enjoys only ten days sunshine a year. Similarly your illustration may assume 9% growth for a fund which has struggled to reach 6%.

You will also have recourse to the Fact Find should a mistake be made. If the adviser skimps on the questions, or doesn't listen to your answers, you may be able to argue that the product has been **missold** and you should have compensation. But if you skimp on the answers, you have only got yourself to blame, and that can be expensive.

The rules require this exhaustive research, even when it is obvious to both adviser and client that it is unnecessary. It is rather like the travel agent looking at the would-be holiday maker and thinking 'Tenerife' or 'Torquay', but having to describe a world cruise and a trek over the Taklamakan desert before he can make the booking.

So if you're in a hurry, be patient with your agent. Consumers can't have it both ways. If you don't want thorough, tailor-made and appropriate advice, skip even the best adviser and go DIY.

HOW TO DIY BUY

Everyone knows that there is a right way and a wrong way to buy DIY home furniture. The wrong way is to purchase something that looks brilliant in the showroom, and afterwards find it comes in 109 self-assembly sections with instructions in Korean. There is also a right and wrong way to purchase financial products.

The Wrong Way

A common mistake is to buy because of an advertisement. Financial services ads take one small positive quality and wrap it in romance, security and/or comedy. Bluffers, who are able to distinguish chicanery from reality, are unlikely to fall for this.

Things to watch out for include:

1. Companies which make a fuss about their long-term performance. They have probably done really badly recently.
2. Those which celebrate last year's spectacular results. This suggests a twelve month blip, rather than a sustainable future.
3. Comparisons with 'other funds in this sector', rather than the market as a whole. The sector may have been a disaster – why should you bail it out?
4. Funds compared to the 'average'. Almost every investment product comes in a thousand varieties – there are over 17,000 unit trusts, for example. So an above-average product can still be out-performed by thousands.
5. The word 'first'. Check whether it means 'first quartile' – the top 25% of funds in the sector. But if there are 500 funds altogether, more than a hundred might make a better home for your money.

The Right Way

Follow the old military three-step approach: reconnoitre, raid and review.

1. Reconnoitre

Rather than ads, rely on independent reviews of the fund or product's performance. Check out:

- The financial press, including the personal finance sections of the weekend papers.
- The public library, with its wide range of magazines on savings, pensions, mortgages and loans. This is your reward for investing in council tax.
- Parties. People love talking about their financial success, but their friends are too envious to listen.

One secret is not just to search for the magic product, the gold at the end of the rainbow. Read widely, and get a feel for what is normal and expected. This will make you both more cynical and more reasonable. It will also teach you newly-minted jargon, invaluable for bluffing.

2. Raid

Raids can be ambushed. If you do your own research, decide what you want, bypass all financial advisers and go straight to the company, you'll fall into a trap. The company won't pay you the adviser's commission – but they'll take charges out of your policy as if they had. So the winner is the institution, not you.

To ensure that you keep the benefits of DIY, you need to:

1. Go direct. Some companies sell straight to the public, without using agents. As a result they charge less. But if a company both sells direct and uses agents,

be careful. Sometimes they charge the same, in order not to upset the advisers. So you think you've got a better deal, but you've been out-bluffed.

2. Use an **execution-only** agent, who acts as your intermediary but without providing any advice. He will either pass you all the commission in exchange for a one-off fee, or else split it with you. If the adviser Mafia had its way, execution-only agents would be terminated.

3. Use an ordinary agent, but say you will only buy if he splits the commission. This is the pragmatic 'half a loaf' principle of financial advice.

If you do a **commission split**, don't just consider the textbook half-and-half version. There are other possible positions:

- Unequal shares. If you're on top, you can ask for more.
- **Renewals**. Most advisers only split the initial commission, which is usually paid in the early months or years of a policy. Subsequently they receive a smaller sum, called renewals, for the rest of the policy term. Although these amounts are small, they are regular, mount up over time, and should not be overlooked. If the adviser wants to retain the renewals, use this as a bargaining counter to get a bigger share up front.
- Extra value. If the adviser gives up his commission, the company has fewer costs. So the adviser can ask the company to **enhance** your policy, i.e. give it more value. So you get a bigger, better policy.
- Cheaper price. Instead of receiving commission, you can pay less for the policy in the first place.

If you really want to sort the sheep from the goats, ask the adviser to explain the various tax consequences of these different positions.

3. Review

Ask yourself: have I won or lost by going it alone? The advantages of DIY are:

- You will have saved money, so the overall return on your investment will be greater;
- You may have saved time;
- You will have stayed in control and not been persuaded to buy more or differently.

The disadvantages are:

- There are thousands of products, and a good adviser may have found a better one;
- You may have missed some key element of the product, buried in the small print;
- You can't sue yourself.

CHARGES

Some financial products resemble striptease clubs. The charges seem low on the doorstep, but once inside you are snared by unexpected costs. It may even be expensive and difficult to leave – many products have exit charges, while others are front-end loaded. This means that most of the costs come out of the investment at the beginning. So if you cancel your endowment in the first two years, you'll probably get back less than you paid in. In a pension policy this front end loading may hide behind the names **capital units**, **initial units** or **initial allocation period**. You don't need to understand how they work, the result is to make more money out of your investment in its early years.

The only solution is to research the charges thoroughly before you enter. Ask if there are:

- Initial charges – for starting the investment.
- Annual management charges – for looking after your money.
- Fees – for using another investment vehicle to hold your money, such as a unit or investment trust.
- Any other costs, including hidden and mislabelled ones such as capital units.
- Bid-offer spreads – you buy at the higher price, but when you sell up, you receive the lower price. The difference is the spread, kept by the fund manager so his bread is buttered on both sides.

Other traps include **low allocation rates** when the company only allocates say 95% your investment to the fund, and pockets the rest. Then there are products which advertise a high income but take all **charges out of capital**, so when you get your original investment back it is less than you expected.

And don't be misled by thinking the charges sound small. They are usually a percentage of the whole sum invested. A 5% annual charge on a £10,000 investment takes £500 a year of your money – so your lump sum has to grow by more than 5% (after tax) simply to stand still. Fund performance tables comparing the results of different products are thus meaningless unless they are 'net of charges'. Always look at the very tiny print.

Another complexity is the link with commission. You don't pay the commission itself – you pay charges, but these are fixed to be high enough to reward the agents. If you start a 20 year endowment policy, an adviser may receive the equivalent of one year's premiums as his commission. So at the end of the first year the charges are likely to have wiped out your premiums – just to pay commission.

Companies are endlessly inventive over charges, as this is how they make their profits. You can only be really sure you know what is going to hit you if you write and ask the company to confirm that:

a) there will be no other charges other than those you are listing
b) they can't increase these after you have bought the product.

This is the best body armour a bluffer can brandish.

Cashbacks

Cashbacks are the opposite of charges. With a cashback, the seller pays you for buying his product rather than someone else's. Sounds too good to be true? Often, but not always, it is.

Some are just disguised price reductions or old-fashioned discounts, repackaged as cashbacks. You will pay for others in more subtle ways – by being locked into a mortgage for a ten year period, when they are able to charge you higher rates than are available in the market.

And beware of the wordmongering which spreads like rumour through financial services – this sort of cashback is not the same as using your **debit card** to obtain cash at a supermarket checkout. That is simply another way of extracting money from your own bank account.

To succeed with cashbacks you need to find the exceptions – such as one given by new players in the market who want to build their customer base by enticing you from your old supplier. They then rely on inertia to hold you once you have transferred. So don't just lie back and think of the last cashback. Find a better one and move on.

GLOSSARY

APR – Abbreviation for April, or for Annual Percentage Rate, the true interest rate on a loan. Not to be confused with CAR (Compounded Annual Rate) the real rate on a savings account or EAR (Effective Annual Rate) on an overdraft. Knowing your CAR from your EAR is the financial equivalent of knowing your ass from your elbow.

Base rate – The interest rate set by the Bank of England, on which other banks base their lending. Like a keynote in music but less creative.

Carpetbaggers – People who join a mutual company hoping it will demutualise and pay out bonuses. Denounced as shameless opportunists by everyone else, i.e. those who already belong and those who left it too late.

Capital – Money, usually a lump sum, which you already own, as distinct from interest which is the reward for investing capital. Losing it can be excruciatingly final, as in capital punishment.

Direct debits – Arrangement for creditors to take money out of your bank account. Suitable for bills which vary in amount. Contrast standing orders when creditors take a fixed sum. Although both are authorised to plunder your current account, unexpected raids can create havoc and overdrafts.

Debit card – Personalised plastic which debits your account sooner than you expect. Hence swipe, switch and swizz.

Direct – No branch, no counter, just a telephone. Some have 24-hour access so you can hear the full Ring Cycle while waiting to be answered.

Enterprise Zone Trust – An EZT is a tax shelter based on property investment. At least as risky as AZT but less therapeutic.

Financial adviser – Politically correct name for a person who sells savings products, just as dustmen are refuse disposal operatives.

Fund manager – Person who makes his money by investing yours.

Fund management company – Company which takes a share of your money and invests the little that's left.

Gross – Return on your investment before the taxman nets his share.

High Net Worth Individuals – Advisers' jargon for rich people. The poor are Ds & Es. If you are categorised F or below, this Xplains Y advisers R not Qing to see U. Penury is its own reward.

Impaired life – Expected to die sooner than average because of disease, inheritance or unhealthy pleasures.

Key Features – Identikit for a financial product, computer enhanced to prevent all products looking like thugs.

Mutual – Organisation, such as a building society or insurance company, owned by its savers. An endangered species, now preserved by mutual admiration societies.

OPRA – Occupational Pensions Regulatory Authority. Speaks loudly in a foreign language and has many supporters or buffs (not bluffs).

Policyholder – Person who has bought a product from an insurance company.

Product – Anything bought from a financial services company. Like a hologram, gives a misleading impression of tangible reality.

Redress – Compensation, e.g. that paid to victims of pensions misselling. Has stripped the industry down to its underwear, some of which is still being washed in public.

Regulators – Those who supervise the fresh air added to financial products.

Term – Length of time (a) money is invested in a financial product or (b) offenders remain behind bars. It's easier to escape from prison, than to recover your capital before the end of the term.

Tied agents – Those who sell the financial products of only one company, which binds them hand and foot.

Transfer Club – Public sector workers moving from one job to another take their pension rights with them, and on retirement are treated as if they had always worked for that employer. This is the government's reward for those in the club.

Will – Your single most important financial planning project. It stops you dying intestate, a painful condition which diverts your assets according to a government formula. As a last resort, your money goes to the Crown. This fact should make even nihilists plan ahead.

Wrapper – Outer layer of financial product which increases its attraction but doesn't change the wafer underneath.

THE AUTHOR

Anne Gordon is a specialist in financial products in the City of London. As a child she put her pocket money in a jam-jar and became, over time, a very good saver. This early discipline now takes the form of cutting out and remembering to use money-off vouchers, and unfailingly checking her bank statements.

She believes passionately that small investors, such as herself, should get a fair deal, or better still make enormous profits. She is still working out the best way to achieve this without risking all her savings on the races, the lottery or the stock market.

Although old enough to know that money talks, she is still young enough to hope that one day she will understand what it says.